TRUE HAPPINESS

Because you are but a young man, beware of temptations and snares; and above all, be careful to keep yourself in the use of means; resort to good company; and howbeit you be nicknamed a Puritan, and mocked, yet care not for that, but rejoice and be glad, that they who are scorned and scoffed by this godless and vain world, and nicknamed Puritans, would admit you to their society; for I must tell you, when I am at this point as you see me, I get no comfort to my soul by any second means under heaven but from those who are nicknamed Puritans. They are the men that can give a word of comfort to a wearied soul in due season, and that I have found by experience . . .

THE LAST AND HEAVENLY SPEECHES, AND
GLORIOUS DEPARTURE, OF JOHN, VISCOUNT KENMURE

THE WAY TO TRUE HAPPINESS

Ralph Venning

THE BANNER OF TRUTH TRUST

THE BANNER OF TRUTH TRUST
3 Murrayfield Road, Edinburgh EH12 6EL, UK
P.O. Box 621, Carlisle, PA 17013, USA

*

© Banner of Truth Trust 2013

ISBN
Print: 978 1 84871 288 1
EPUB: 978 1 84871 289 8
Kindle: 978 1 84871 290 4

*

Typeset in 10.5/13.5 pt Adobe Caslon Pro
at the Banner of Truth Trust, Edinburgh

Printed in the USA by
Versa Press, Inc.,
East Peoria, IL

INTRODUCTION

ALTHOUGH less well known to twenty-first century readers than his associates Richard Baxter and John Owen, or contemporaries such as John Bunyan, Ralph Venning was not only highly respected and 'much followed' by fellow Puritans during his own lifetime, but his influence has continued to resonate across the centuries. Baxter, for example, described him as a 'godly, orthodox' preacher, while the Puritan biographer and pastor, Edmund Calamy, admired his ability of evoking generosity and charitable compassion on behalf of the poor even from the most miserly individual. Later biographers shared Baxter's appreciation of his 'moderation', and identified Venning as a 'man of no particular faction' during the turbulent period of disunity among believers—a man who sought the unity of God's people in their shared pursuit of godliness or 'Godlikeness.'

Venning's writings continued to be published on both sides of the Atlantic throughout the eighteenth and nineteenth centuries, with something of a revival of interest in the late 1800s. They continue to inspire evangelical believers today. His most popular writings were his aphorisms or pithy, proverbial sayings which affirmed the truths of the Christian faith and presented them in a style that was easily and intentionally memorable by his readers. Venning published a number of such works between 1647 and 1665 including his two-part *Milk and Honey*, and *Things Worth Thinking On*.

However, Venning's treatises on the Christian life, developed from sermons he had preached, also continue to appeal to evangelical readers. In particular, *The Plague of Plagues* (1669) and *Christ's School* (1675) have both been published by the Banner of Truth Trust under the titles *The Sinfulness of Sin* and *Learning in Christ's School* respectively.[1] These works, as do Venning's other writings, challenge the reader to pursue godliness in every aspect of daily life, following Christ ever more closely.

Who was Ralph Venning?

Ralph Venning was born in Devon around the year 1621 to Francis and Joanne Venning,

---

[1] See advertisement pages at end of book for more details.

and spent his childhood and early adult life in the vicinity of Tavistock, where his father was a yeoman farmer. There Venning encountered the Puritan preacher, George Hughes, under whose diligent pastoral ministry he was converted, along with two other young men who also went on to become gospel ministers. Venning later acknowledged the debt he owed to Hughes, whose devotion of time and energy both to Venning's conversion and early discipleship, led to him describing Hughes in affectionate terms as his spiritual 'father'.

His academic and, perhaps, ministerial potential having been recognised, Venning left Devon for Cambridge. He was admitted to Emmanuel College as a 'sizar' in April 1643—a category of student which would have required him to carry out menial jobs around the college in part payment of his fees. Despite these additional duties—he also served as chaplain in the Tower of London, and found the time to write and publish two books—Venning completed his BA and MA degrees before entering into the preaching ministry.

Apart from a short period in Devon, Venning ministered primarily in London, in fellowship with both Independent and Presbyterian preachers such as Joseph Caryl, John Owen, Richard Baxter and George Griffith. Indeed, London was a hub for godly preaching at that time. Venning, although known for his moderation and as one who avoided partisanship, was unequivocally committed to the goals of the Reformation and of the 'Puritan revolution', and served in a number of capacities during the Commonwealth period and under the Protectorate of Oliver Cromwell. These included the Commissions for assessing candidates for chaplaincy posts in the navy and for the County of Surrey, as well as promoting evangelical enterprise amongst the indigenous peoples of New England. Of greatest importance to Venning, however, was the promotion of godliness in every aspect of daily life.

During the 1650s Venning was primarily occupied as Lecturer at St Olave's, Southwark. The church was fully demolished by 1928, and Olaf House, part of London Bridge Hospital, now occupies the spot. Refusing to conform to the 1662 Act of Uniformity, Venning was ejected from this post. In the years that followed, he ministered to a nonconformist congregation which met at the Pewterers' Guild Hall in Lime Street. His last sermon, after which he was taken ill and died (March 1674), was preached to a similar congregation meeting at Joiners' Hall.

In addition to his ministry among the Reformed churches during the heady days of the 1650s, Venning also preached on occasions at Paul's Cross, an open air pulpit adjacent to St Paul's Cathedral, and described by historian Patrick Collinson as the seventeenth century equivalent of national broadcasting. Those who listened would have included the Aldermen and Mayor of London, as well as a broad spectrum of both Londoners and visitors to the capital. This was a platform to present to the widest possible audience sermons on matters of national importance. *The Way to True Happiness* was one such sermon.

The Way to True Happiness

When C. H. Spurgeon sought a fitting quotation from the Puritan authors for his own sermons on the believer's happiness, it was to Venning in particular that he turned. Indeed, the certainty that true happiness is to be found in God alone is central to

Venning's treatment of this subject. This is reflected in his sermon *The Way To True Happiness, or The Way to Heaven Open'd.*

First preached on 28 January 1655,[2] the sermon was published by John Rothwell at the request of the Lord Mayor, Christopher Packe, having been edited by Venning for the press. In it Venning proposes that none of the world's apparent pleasures could fully satisfy the individual or make him truly happy. Ultimate happiness can be found only in God himself—just as Augustine had acknowledged over a thousand years previously: 'You made us for yourself and our souls are restless until they find their rest in you.'

The means to attain true happiness is through a relationship with God, made

[2] In Venning's time, the calendar year was reckoned as starting on Lady Day (25 March), although for the purpose of this book dates have been calculated according to modern usage.

possible by God's grace alone through faith in his Son, Jesus Christ. This relationship can be enjoyed in every aspect of one's daily life through obedience to God's commandments—obedience which is itself a fruit of grace. The commandments of God are not 'burdensome', or 'grievous' as Venning would have read 1 John 5:3, but rather are given by a good and loving God so that people might avoid the pain and misery which must always be the consequences of sin.

For Venning, faith in Christ changes everything—personal life and the community in which the believer lives. Venning was an example of such gospel transformation. He was not only admired for his preaching but also for the consistency of his life—his personal godliness with the message he preached. This combination of life and lip, together with his powerful calls to a pleasure-obsessed world to seek happiness only where it may be truly found, are perhaps the reasons why his writings continue to speak so powerfully to us today.

S. Bryn Roberts
Glasgow, June 2013

Note on Language

In this edition, English spellings have been updated as have some of Venning's seventeenth century idioms, while quotations from Latin sources have been translated for the benefit of the reader unfamiliar with the language. The text, however, remains substantially Venning's and has not been abridged. Direct quotations from Scripture are in the Authorised, or King James Version, commonly used by Venning, however, where he has translated the text differently and this has been deemed essential to his purpose, his translation has been preserved.

The Epistle Dedicatory:

TO the Right Honourable Christopher Packe, Lord Mayor, and the Right Worshipful Aldermen of the City of London—

That I print this sermon, and that I have expanded upon it, is in obedience to your order, which, having resolved a former scruple of mine, gave me warrant for so doing—and I hope that the reader's advantage will also be the greater. My preaching then was not—nor my writing now—with the enticing words of man's wisdom but, I hope, in the evidence and demonstration of the Spirit and power. The reason is that your faith should not stand upon the wisdom of words, but in the words of wisdom; or, as the apostle phrases it, not in the wisdom of men, but in the power of God, in order that the heavenly treasure might not taste of the earthen vessel (cf. *1 Cor.* 2:4).

Certainly there was never more need than in our days of preaching and pressing that command of our blessed Saviour, 'Labour not' or 'work not' for 'the meat which perisheth, but for that meat which endureth unto everlasting life' (cf. *John* 6:27). And if any say to me as they did to him, 'What shall we do that we may work the Work of God?' I refer them to the following discourse for their answer; concerning which I only desire that the Scriptures may be searched which abundantly witness to it. 'To the Law and to the Testimony:' if it does not speak according to that rule, there is no light in it. If it appears, as I believe it will, to be the voice of God, and not of man, I hope that none will quarrel with it, that they may not be found fighters against God. And why would we provoke the Lord to jealousy unless we were stronger than he is?

Solomon tells us that of making and reading many books there is no end, and when we have read—if we could read—all that have ever been written, this would be the conclusion of the whole matter, 'Fear God and keep his commandments.' For this is the whole (we read it 'duty' but it is rightly translated simply as 'whole') contentment and happiness of man. This is all that is profitable to man, it being opposed to everything else that is under the sun, which is but vanity and vexation of spirit. Truly, 'we may as well find ease in hell' as find happiness any other way—just as we shall know (whatever we may think now) when God shall bring every work into judgement, with every secret thing, whether it be good or evil.[3]

How much then does it concern us to look about us: to work out our salvation with fear and trembling here, that we may not fear and tremble *then*, because we had not done so *now*? Therefore, knowing the fear of the Lord we persuade men—as they love their salvation and as they will answer for it at the great and terrible day of the righteous judgement of God—that they keep themselves from the lusts of the flesh

---

[3] Venning quotes here, although not verbatim, from a poem by Francis Quarles. Cf. F. Quarles, *Emblemes* (Cambridge: Francis Eglesfield, 1643), p. 13. Quarles' original reads:

> Alas fond Child,
> How are thy thoughts beguil'd,
> To hope for honey from a nest of wasps?
> Thou mayst as well
> Go seek for ease in hell,
> Or sprightly Nectar from the mouths of asps.

which war against their souls; that they lean not on their own understanding, nor walk in the ways of their own hearts and the desires of their eyes. Rather, that they might consider to know and to do what is the good and acceptable will of God so that they may be found without blame. And when he appears, you also may have confidence and not be ashamed before him at his coming.

Watch, then, for you do not know at what hour your Lord will come. If any servant says in his heart, 'My Lord delayeth his coming' (*Matt.* 24:48; *Luke* 12:45) and beats his fellow servants and eats and drinks with those who are drunk, the Lord of that servant will come in a day when he is not looking for him, and at an hour when he is not aware. He will cut that servant in pieces —he will 'cut him off'— and appoint him his portion with unbelievers. That servant which knew his Lord's will, and did not prepare or do his will, shall be beaten 'with many stripes.'[4]

I hope that none will say, as did that man who had a book brought to him about happiness, 'I'm not at leisure' or 'I don't have time.' What? Not at leisure to think of your soul and your happiness? Are the world and sin such excellent pieces? Are they so lovely that you would set your heart on them? Oh, why would you set your eyes upon that which is nothing? It is not what it seems to be—it is not what you need nor what you think it to be. Indeed, it will prove the greatest cheat that there can be and though you gain the whole world, what profit will it be to you if you lose your soul?

Well, you see the world tottering and tumbling about your ears: the fashion of it, the lustre of it—oh that it was true of the

[4] Luke 12:47

lust *for* it!—will pass away. We ourselves are making haste towards our grave—if these things are not taken from us, we shall nevertheless be taken from them! And who knows (only God knows) how soon. Today, then, let us hear and obey the voice of God that when the Lord comes, he may find us so doing as to say to us, 'Well done, good and faithful servants: enter into your Master's joy; Come, you who are blessed of my Father, inherit the Kingdom.'[5]

That this may be your portion, and the portion of those who heard it, and of those who read it, is the heartfelt prayer of

RALPH VENNING
20 February 1655

[5] cf. Matthew 25:21, 34

THE WAY TO
TRUE HAPPINESS

Not every one that saith unto me, Lord, Lord, shall enter into the kingdom of heaven; but he that doeth the will of my Father which is in heaven (Matt. 7:21).

THOUGH there is nothing more natural to man, than to seek after happiness, yet there is nothing that the nature of man is less able to find out than what will bring him happiness. Man's hungering desire to attain happiness is not abated, though his ability for its attainment (by himself), is utterly lost. Since he ate the forbidden fruit—that is, since he sinned—ever since he was banished from the well-watered garden of God, he (poor man!) has wandered up and down like a fugitive in the land of Nod, seeking rest in dry places, but finding none. Alas, how is poor, silly man bewildered in the pursuit of his chief good! He walks in darkness, and does not know where he is going—he stumbles and falls. In seeking to save himself, he loses himself.

It is with him as it was with the blinded men of Sodom, who, though groping to find the door, went further from it; or like the dove, when it left the ark, always upon the wing, ever flying and fluttering, but never finding where to place the sole of her foot. Just so is it with man since he left God: he knows not where to rest the foot of his soul. Now here, now there, he goes; forward and then back again; to the right and to the left to see if he can find out what is good for the souls of the sons of men (like Job in another case and Solomon in this same matter of happiness). All this exertion is to find that which they should do under heaven all the days of their life, so that after this life of days is ended, they may enjoy eternal life with God in heaven. But alas, I must say it again, man is still at a loss!

Now seeing that man was in this pitifully sad and miserable condition, it pleased God (who is a lover of the souls—and the preserver—of men), in tender mercy to mankind, to speak at many different times (or by piece-meal), and in different ways to the fathers by the prophets; but in the fullness of time to send, and in these last days to speak to us, by his Son. He has declared his will fully and wholly by him, so that we need not look for another, there being no name under heaven but his by which we can be saved. Where then should we go for the discovery (seeing he only has the words) of eternal life? Him, I say, God has sent to guide our feet into the way of peace, that he might be the way, and the truth, and the life unto us. He sent Christ from heaven to earth that Christ might send men from earth to heaven.

Christ has acquitted himself accordingly like a faithful steward—he has finished the work which his Father gave him to do. He has done and suffered all that was commanded him for the good of men. He is therefore pure from the blood of all men, having declared unto them the whole counsel of God, and chalked out the way in which they are to walk that they may be happy. He has given us the sum of this in our text, and that is the doing of his Father's will.

The Text:

Christ Jesus, having exhorted them in verse

13 to enter in (or, as Luke expounds it in chapter 13, verse 24, to 'strive to enter in') at the narrow gate, with powerful arguments to encourage them to do so, advises them in verse 15 to beware of false prophets that they might not be misled in a business of such great importance to them. Therefore he tells them in verse 16 (repeated in verse 20) how they may know them, that is, by their fruits: by their *works* not by their words. They may speak as others do, so that they may not be known by their words, but, Christ says, by their fruits you shall know them. Having said this, he sets out as of the greatest concern to all: 'Not every one that saith Lord, Lord . . .'

I shall open up this text a little and then draw out the central point which I intend to expound.

Not every one, that is, not any one. Not every one is as much as if he had said, *no not one*. It is a universal negative, without exception. Not any one that says and does not do—that says, 'I'll go' but doesn't go; who says and *only* says, 'Lord, Lord'. This may be understood in three respects. 'Not every one' that says, 'Lord, Lord' by way of:

1. Profession.
2. Prayer.
3. Appeal.

1. Profession:

Not every one that says, 'Lord, Lord' by way of profession, that professes me to be his Lord. As in John 13:13, 'Ye call me Lord and Master, and ye do well'—that is, so far you do well—'for so I am.' However, if I am your Lord and Master, where is the honour I am due? Or as he says, 'Why call ye me Lord, Lord, and do not the things which I say?' Why? That is to say, to what end and purpose? None! In vain do you profess me to be your Lord, unless you are obedient to me, your Lord. It is not profession but practice that matters—at least not profession without practice. It will not do any man any good to be but a pretender to religion.

He that confesses Christ in words and in works denies him, has but a form of godliness without the power. Such a man will not be proved righteous by his good words but condemned by his bad works. What will it avail to have the reputation of being alive, but to be dead while we live? To have the name of a Christian and not to be as our name is? Many ships have had the name *Safeguard* or *Goodspeed,* yet have foundered. Many men have had a good name and yet have made a bad end, a very bad end—indeed, who have been punished with everlasting destruction, away from the presence of him whom they have called 'Lord, Lord'. Not every one that saith Lord, Lord shall enter the kingdom of heaven.

2. *Prayer:*

Not every one that says, 'Lord, Lord', by way of prayer, as they did in Matthew 25:11: 'Lord, Lord, open to us.' Though it is truly said that every one that calls on the name of the Lord shall be saved, yet you see that a man may call upon the name of the Lord—and that again and again he may call Lord, Lord—and yet be damned. His repetitions will be in vain, because they are *vain repetitions*. A man may add prayers to his profession, and yet despite all his professions and prayers he may go to hell. For, not every one who says Lord, Lord, either by way of profession, or prayer, or both, shall enter the kingdom of heaven.

3. *Appeal:*

Not every one that says, 'Lord, Lord', by way of appeal, as in verse 22: 'Many shall say to me in that day, Lord, Lord, have we not prophesied in your name?' 'Have we not? We make our appeal to you, we call you to witness and make you our judge.' Thus the name of the Lord is often called upon—too often called upon—as by those in Jeremiah 42:5.[6] The Lord, they say, is witness between you and us. Appeals made for justification do not always justify, nor are they justified. Jeremiah says to them, 'You did at that time'—at that very time—'when you appealed to God, dissemble in your hearts.' At this time, Christ says similarly, though you say unto me, 'Lord, Lord', by way of

---

[6] 'Then they said to Jeremiah, The LORD be a true and faithful witness between us, if we do not even according to all things for the which the LORD thy God shall send thee to us' (*Jer.* 42:5). The following reference to Jeremiah 42:20 is a paraphrase rather than a direct quotation.

appeal, yet I profess I never knew you, I never approved of you: Depart from me you workers of iniquity! So, it is not profession, prayer, or appeal alone that will give a man entrance into the kingdom of heaven.

By 'the kingdom of heaven' is to be understood that state of blessedness after this life, called elsewhere salvation, glory and eternal life; which indeed is begun in this life for, 'This is life eternal, to know thee the only true God, and Jesus Christ whom thou hast sent' (*John* 17:3). Therefore the dispensation of grace by Jesus Christ is often called the kingdom of heaven—'Repent for the kingdom of heaven is at hand.' I think the future state is principally meant here, for: 'Then shall the righteous shine forth as the sun in the kingdom of their Father' (*Matt.* 13:43).

Before I move on to the second clause in this verse I shall make some observations from the text and its context.

From the connection of this text with the previous verse, I shall observe that men are better known by what they do than by what they say. Even a child, Solomon says, is known by his actions (*Prov.* 20:11)— whether his work is pure and right. So says Christ, 'By their fruits ye shall know them.' Not every one that says Lord, Lord will enter the kingdom of heaven. Rather, men are better known by their doings than by their sayings. If a man speaks well but does ill, charity itself cannot speak well of that man.

As regards men, God indeed judges their words and their works by their hearts, but men cannot judge of men except by their works. 'By their fruits ye shall know them.' Not by their *profession*—for they may profess like saints; nor by their *prayers*—for they may pray like saints; nor by their *appeals*— for they may appeal like saints. They may say,

'Lord, Lord' but 'by their fruits ye shall know them.' It is not the words but the works of men that tell us what they are. Indeed, says Christ, they come to you in sheep's clothing but they are ravening wolves. They have Jacob's smooth tongue but Esau's rough hand. They speak like angels of light but they act like angels of darkness. They defy the devil in words but deify him in works; they deify Christ in words but defy him in works. God does not like the 'court holy-water'[7] of fair professions of faith and deep expressions of devotion, when men's hearts are not with him—when there is not the power of religion, and the practice of godliness. 'By their fruits ye shall know them.' Not every one who says, 'Lord, Lord' shall enter the kingdom of heaven. Furthermore:

[7] An expression meaning fine promises made without any intention of keeping them. It occurs also in Shakespeare's *King Lear,* Act III, Scene II.

1. Good words without good works will never give a good account—holy sayings without holy doings will never admit into the holy place. Not every one who says, 'Lord, Lord' shall enter the kingdom of heaven.

2. God is a very interested observer of what men say and of what men do in the world. Jesus Christ observes here that they say, 'Lord, Lord' but declares also that they do not do the will of his Father, but are workers of iniquity. Men indeed may, but God will not—God cannot—be fooled by appearances. Shall not he that made the eye, see? Shall not he that made the ear, hear? Shall not he that made the heart, know what is in it? 'Surely,' says David, 'Thou understandest my thoughts', and 'there is not a word in my tongue, but lo, thou knowest it altogether' (*Psa.* 139:4). And, as for works, as Christ says to the Church of

Ephesus: 'I know thy works' (*Rev.* 2:2).

Moving on, I'll proceed now to the second clause: 'He that doeth the will of my Father which is in heaven.' From this I conclude that they, and none but they, who do the will of God, shall enter into the kingdom of heaven. To clarify this we must ask: What are we to understand by the 'will' and by 'doing the will' of God? Having answered these questions, we may more safely proceed to test the truth of our proposition. However, before doing so, I must premise these two things:

1. That the will of God the Father, and his Son, Jesus Christ, are one. The Father and he are one, and agree in one, and indeed, it is in him and by him that we know the will of God. 'No man', says John, 'hath seen God at any time; the only begotten Son which is in the bosom of the Father, he hath declared him' (*John* 1:18). And as the

apostle says, 'Who hath known the mind of the Lord? But we have the mind of Christ' (*1 Cor.* 2:16), by which we have the mind of God. The Father says of the Son as Pharaoh did of Joseph, 'Go unto Joseph: what he saith unto you, do' (*Gen.* 41:55); and as Christ's mother said to the servants at the wedding, 'Whatsoever he saith unto you, do it' (*John* 2:5). In the same way his Father says, 'This is my beloved Son in whom I am well pleased, hear ye him' (*Matt.* 17:5). So, whatever Christ says to you is his Father's will and therefore he calls them 'his sayings' (verse 24), and pronounces them blessed who hear and do them, for they are his Father's will.

2. As to the terms used I premise this also: these expressions such as the will of God, the word of God, the work of God, the commandments of God, *etc.*, are all equivalent and signify the same thing.

So then, by the will of God, we are to understand:

1. The *Credenda,* or Faith.

2. The *Agenda,* which is Holiness.

Not either, but each of them; not one or the other, but both one and the other. The doctrine of faith or things to be believed; and the doctrine of holiness or things to be done and practised. Just as faith does not exclude action, so action does not exclude faith; for as faith without works is dead, so works without faith are dead also. Just as it is impossible that faith without works can please God, so it is no less impossible for works without faith to please God. 'Therefore what God hath joined together, man should not separate'.[8]

You shall find that believing is expressly

[8] *Mark* 10:9. Venning combines the translations of the King James and Geneva Versions of the verse: though primarily he quotes from the KJV. His point is that faith is 'married' to good works in the Christian life.

called the will of God in John 6:27: 'Labour not', says Christ, 'for the meat which perisheth, but for that which endureth unto everlasting life, which the Son of man shall give unto you.' From this we observe that God's giving and man's labouring are not inconsistent: free grace and full duty may join hearts and hands. But, they say in verse 28, 'What shall we do, that we may work the works of God?' Jesus answered and said 'This is the work (that is, the will of God) that ye believe on him whom he hath sent' (verse 29). In the same way, in verse 40: 'This is the will of him that sent me, that every one that believeth on the Son, should have everlasting life.' Now if this is his will, that believing on him we have everlasting life, then it is also his will that we believe on Christ. So then, believing on him for everlasting life is the will of God. Indeed, you have it expressly in 1 John 3:23: 'This is his commandment that we should believe on the name of his Son Jesus Christ.' So you see, it is not only that which we usually call good works that is to be understood as 'doing the will of God,' but believing in or on the Lord Jesus Christ also. This is the *work*, this is the *will*, this is the *command* of God.

Beloved, I'll strengthen my case still further by noting the following principle, which is an undeniable one; and by not giving it our attention we have had so many needless, groundless, and unprofitable disputes in the world. The principle is this: that the Scriptures often—indeed, usually—put particular duties for the whole of religion, and therefore they associate salvation with distinct graces. Sometimes it is 'He that believes shall be saved'; elsewhere, 'He that calls upon the name of the Lord shall be saved.' Here it is, 'He that doeth the will of

God.' Now, all these and the like are complex and comprehensive propositions and contain more in them than they show—for God speaks much in a little. Acts and duties of religion are linked together in a golden chain. Religion is not this or that piece, but the *whole*, although it is usually expressed in a word or two, as in Solomon's statement of it: 'Fear God, and keep his commandments, for this is the whole duty of man (*Eccles.* 12:13). So that if you could suppose a man to be a believer, and to be a believer alone, it would not save him as the Apostle James says (*James* 2:14): 'What doth it profit, my brethren, though a man say he hath faith, and have not works? can faith save him?' No. No more than saying, 'Be warm', will warm anyone or 'Be filled', will fill anyone, for faith without works is dead.

And what is said of this case may be said of the rest, so that when the Scriptures speak of salvation as connected to any one thing, it supposes it to contain all the rest. The reason is evident: the graces of God in saving are not separate. There is no believing for salvation without repentance, nor repentance without believing; there is no calling upon the name of the Lord will save without departing from sin, nor can they depart from sin without calling on the name of the Lord. It is not any one thing that pertains to the kingdom of God but 'things' (*Acts* 1:3). It is not one thing, but 'things' that accompany salvation (*Heb.* 6:9), and he who takes one for all without all, will find it worth nothing at all.

The great fallacy with which Satan deludes many men is that by which he gets them to take religion to pieces, and then take only one piece for religion. One cries up God, another cries up Christ, another faith, another love, another good works; but what is God without Christ, or Christ without faith, or faith without love, or love without works? Instead, take God in Christ, by faith which works by love to the keeping of the commandments of God, and this is pure religion. It is the whole, and the wholeness of man.

Yet again, though I have said this much about it, let me make it clearer, that one is put for all, and as containing all, by comparing these places of Scripture. In 1 Corinthians 7:19 you read that circumcision is nothing and uncircumcision is nothing, but keeping the commandments of God is what counts. What's that? Why, that is all in all. In Galatians 5:6, it is neither circumcision nor uncircumcision, but 'faith which worketh by love' that avails or is all in all. Yet in Galatians 6:15 he says, 'neither circumcision availeth any thing, nor uncircumcision, but a new creature' that is all in all. And yet for all this, as if all this were nothing, he tells us in Colossians 3:11, that 'Christ is all and in all', cashiering[9] both circumcision and uncircumcision, as before.

Now, my beloved, if you should take any one of these, though each is said to be 'availing', and lay the stress of your salvation upon it, you would be undone. It is not keeping the commandments of God, nor faith working by love, nor the new creation, no, nor Christ himself considered alone and apart that avails anything, but these in conjunction. He names only one of these in each case, but there is more than one. Wherever one is savingly present, there are all the others in their respective places. Thus you see that faith as well as works, and works as well as faith (every one in its own order) are to be taken in, or we shall not be taken into the kingdom of heaven. And this

[9] dismissing.

will suffice for the opening of that point.

Proving the point:

As to the proof of this, I might say that Christ himself has said it, and what need is there of any further witnesses, seeing we know and are assured that his witness is true? Yet I shall give you a whole cloud of witnesses—the harmony and consent of the Scriptures—to clear up this point, to evidence the truth of this to be past contradiction and without controversy. I shall say nothing of the connection between the two petitions in the Lord's Prayer (*Matt.* 6:10), 'Thy kingdom come', and 'thy will be done'. Nor that in Hebrews 10:36 which states, 'For ye have need of patience, that after ye have done the will of God, ye might receive the promise.' That is, of the kingdom of heaven, or eternal life, for this is the promise which he has made (*1 John* 2:25). I shall also only mention that in 1 John 2:17, it is written, 'He that doeth the will of God abideth for ever.' To prove my case, I shall instead take my evidence:

1. From the testimony that God has given of those already gone to heaven; that they were such people. The first is Enoch, of whom it is said that he walked with God (which is all one, as if it had been said, he did the will of God), and was not—was no longer on earth—for God took him up to heaven (*Gen.* 5:24). This is all that is said of Enoch in the Old Testament, and not one word is mentioned of faith; but that his believing is to be understood is clear from Hebrews 11:5, where we are told the story more fully: 'By faith Enoch was translated that he should not see death; and was not found, because God had translated him: for before his translation he had this testimony, that he pleased God', or as it is in

Genesis, that he walked with God. Now, that he could not walk with, or please God but by faith is fully asserted in verse 6: 'But without faith it is impossible to please him.' And that the faith there spoken of relates to Christ is clear because none can so seek him as to find the reward except by Christ, for none come to the Father except by him. Indeed, that Enoch had special respect to Christ may be gathered from his own prophecy where he says 'Behold the Lord', that is, the Lord Christ, as is apparent by comparing this with 2 Thessalonians 1:7-8. 'The Lord comes with ten thousand of his saints' (*Jude* 14). So, Enoch was a believing walker, or a walking believer, and as such was translated.

The second example is David of whom it is said that God raised him up and gave testimony to him saying, 'I have found David the son of Jesse, a man after mine own heart, who shall fulfil all my wills' (*Acts* 13:22).[10] It is also said of him that after he had served the will of God in his generation he (as to his body) fell asleep. Many men serve their generations by the will of God that do not serve the will of God in their generations, but David served the will of God. Now that David also in serving the will of God acted as a believer is evident from Hebrews 11:32, 33: 'What shall I'—what need is there that I should—'more say? for the time would fail me to tell of Gideon', and others, and of David also: a believer, doing the will of God, who went to heaven.

2. As it appears by the testimony God has given to the persons gone to heaven, so also by the testimony he bears against the persons that are gone, and are to go, to hell.

---

[10] Venning translates 'will' as a plural in keeping with the Greek text.

As in the verse following our text: 'Depart from me ye workers of iniquity.' And again, 'Depart from me all ye workers of iniquity (*Luke* 13:27). Indeed, yet again, 'Depart from me ye cursed into everlasting fire.' Why? 'For I was an hungered and ye gave me no meat.' That is, you did not do my or my Father's will. Now, how does it come to pass that men are workers of iniquity? From unbelief, as becomes clear by comparing a few texts. 'You were dead in trespasses and sins, wherein ye walked, according to the prince of the power of the air,' that is, according to his will, 'who still works in the children of disobedience' (cf. *Eph.* 2:2).

The word is of unbelief: just as good works spring from faith, so bad works spring from unbelief. Their disobedience was of unbelief and 'unbeliever' is as comprehensive a word as 'workers of iniquity,' therefore it is said of those that do not do God's will (*Luke*

12:46): He 'will appoint him his portion with the unbelievers.' And who were they that did not enter into rest but those that did not believe? So we see that they could not enter in because of unbelief (*Heb.* 3:18-19), and due to this unbelief they were workers of iniquity. Thus we have these solemn cautions given to us (*Heb.* 3:12): 'Take heed, brethren, lest there be in any of you an evil heart of unbelief, to depart from the living God;' and again in Hebrews 4:1, 'Let us therefore fear, lest, a promise being left us of entering into his rest, any of you should seem to come short of it,' that is, through unbelief as in verse 11: 'Let us labour therefore to enter into that rest, lest any man fall after the same example of unbelief.' So then you see, beloved, that those who are admitted, believingly do the will of God, and those that are to be shut out are such as work iniquity from unbelief, or do not do the Will of God.

3. Furthermore, it is clear by this, that there can be no works of grace proved powerful and saving but by doing the will of God. For it is said of knowledge, 'He that saith I know him, and keepeth not his commandments is a liar, and the truth is not in him' (*1 John* 2:4): in other words, the truth of that knowledge which he claims to have for the saving of his soul. Likewise in regard to love, the apostle is no less clear in 1 John 5:3: 'This is the love of God that we keep his commandments: and his commandments are not grievous.' The same might be said of the rest, such as faith etc.

Well then, you see that no man has any grounds to expect entrance into the kingdom of heaven, that does not do the will of God; that does not walk with God in faith and obedience, or in the obedience of faith. If anyone should suppose that they may marry the Rachel of heaven, without serving the will of the Father, or before they have married the Leah of obedience, let them know, for God will tell them, as Laban did Jacob: 'It's not the custom of this country to marry the younger before the elder.'[11] But if this that has been said should not be thought sufficient and you need to have further witness, proof and evidence of this truth, I will give you six demonstrations of it from Scripture.

1. No man can enter the kingdom of heaven but he for whom it is prepared. Now, it is prepared for none but them that do the will of God, therefore none but they can enter, and this is asserted by Christ himself. The first proposition is laid down in Matthew 20:23: he says, 'To sit at my right hand, and on my left hand'—in the kingdom as he prayed before—'is not mine to give'—to

---

[11] Genesis 29:26. Venning gives his own translation of the verse, which resembles most closely the Geneva Bible.

any—'but for whom it is prepared of my Father.' The kingdom of heaven is not an inn. It is not open to all, but a particular place for a particular people. And who they are the second proposition tells us: none but they that do the will of God. Christ tells us this himself: 'Then shall the King say to them on his right hand, "Come ye blessed of my Father, inherit the kingdom prepared for you,"' in other words, those who did my Father's will: who fed me when I was hungry, clothed me when I was naked etc. (*Matt.* 25:34). This, as the Apostle James says, is 'pure religion,' undefiled in the sight of God the Father (*James* 1:27).

2. A second demonstration is this: none can enter the kingdom of heaven, but they who are prepared for it; and none are such but they that do the will of God (in the sense explained). Heaven is not only prepared for them, but they are also prepared

for heaven. This world is but a 'Purgatory' for men, that they may be purified and refined here, and thereby enabled (as Esther was in another case) to enter into the kingdom of God, for no unclean thing can enter there. And that we must be made fit to be partakers before we partake, is clear from Colossians 1:12, where the apostle exhorts them (having prayed) that they might give thanks to the Father, who had made them 'meet to be partakers of the inheritance of the saints in light,' who had fitted them for the kingdom of heaven. For that is the inheritance of the saints in light. How that was done, he tells us in verse 13: by delivering us from the 'power of darkness' into 'the kingdom of his dear Son.' A man must be in the kingdom of the Son, which is the kingdom of heaven on Earth, and be thus fitted for—before he can be admitted into—the kingdom of God. This translation is

nothing other than fitting us by enabling us
to do the will of God, for being in the kingdom of Christ is opposed to being under
the power of Satan and therefore must carry
a sense contrary to it. Now, when we were
under that power, we were led by him at his
will (*Eph.* 2:2-3). We were at his beck and
call—his will was our law. Therefore, to be
translated from there into the kingdom of
Christ can denote no less than our obedience to him, or our doing Christ's will, by
which we are made to be partakers of the
inheritance of the saints.

3. A third demonstration is this: none
can enter into the kingdom of heaven but
they to whom it is promised. They that have
no promise can expect no performance. Now,
it is promised to none but such as do the will
of God. 'Hath not (says the apostle), God
chosen the poor of the world, rich in faith,
and heirs of the kingdom, which he hath

promised to them that love him?' (*James* 2:5)
And who they are we have already been told:
those who keep his commandments, and to
whom the keeping of his commandments, or
the doing of his will, is not grievous.

4. A fourth demonstration is this: none
but the friends of God shall inherit the kingdom of God. As for his enemies, who were
not willing that he should reign over them,
they shall never reign with him. 'No', he says,
'bring them forth and slay them before my
face' (cf. *Luke* 19:27). Christ will see execution
done upon his enemies, but as for his friends,
they and none but they shall inherit the
kingdom. Abraham was God's friend, and
Paradise itself is called 'Abraham's bosom'
(*Luke* 16:23). One part of our glorious state
is this: we shall sit down with Abraham the
friend of God (with Isaac and Jacob, and the
rest of the friends of God) in his kingdom.
But who are his friends, then? Christ tells

us in Matthew 12:50: 'Whosoever shall do the will of my Father, which is in heaven,' or (as Mark renders it), 'the will of God;' or (as Luke puts it) 'who hear the Word of God and do it' (which are all parallel expressions), 'the same is my brother, and sister, and mother': my nearest and dearest friends. Yet a more significant place—if it is possible—may be produced, where Christ says to his disciples, 'Ye are my friends, if ye do whatsoever I command you' (*John* 15:14). So then, none but friends can enter, and none are friends but such as do his will.

5. A fifth demonstration is this: none shall enter into the kingdom of heaven, but those that are born again, and none are born again but such as the text mentions—the Scripture is clear upon this. This is set down by Christ himself in John 3:3 with a double 'verily.' 'Verily, verily'—of most certain and undoubted truth—'I say unto thee, except

a man be born again' or 'from above' or, as elsewhere, 'of God', 'he cannot see (which is expounded in verse 5, "unless he be born of water and the Spirit, he cannot enter into") the kingdom of God.' All who are born of God have this character: 'Ye know that every one that's born of him does righteousness' (cf. *1 John* 2:29), and again, 'Whosoever is born of God doth not commit sin ... because he is born of God' (*1 John* 3:9). That is, he does not live in sin, is not under the dominion or command of sin; sin does not reign in him, that he should obey it in its lusts and will.

6. The sixth and last demonstration is this: none can enter into the kingdom of heaven, but holy ones. Hebrews 12:14 says, 'Without holiness no man shall see the Lord.' Now what is holiness, but doing the will of God? 'This is the will of God, even your sanctification' (*1 Thess.* 4:3), and 'He

that hath this hope,' that is, of glory or the kingdom of heaven, 'purifieth himself, even as God is pure' (cf. *1 John* 3:3).

Thus, I think I have fully proved and demonstrated this to be the truth of God according to the Scriptures that they—and none but they—shall enter into the kingdom of heaven, but those who do the will of God. That is, that do believe in the Lord Jesus Christ and produce the obedience of faith.

Who, then, can attain to true happiness?

But, happily, there may be this question raised, 'Who then can be saved?' When Christ had said that it was hard (and it is no less hard in this day) for a rich man to enter into the kingdom of God—they have as much baggage as the camel has in the load on his back, they said, 'Who then can be saved?' The answer given was—and is now:

'The things which are impossible with men are possible,' indeed, very feasible, 'with God' (*Luke* 18:27). But in addition to this let me more distinctly lay down these few points.

1. That all satisfying and all meriting work is done. It is all already done by the Lord Jesus Christ, who offered up himself once for all, and does not need to be offered up again. In burnt offering and sacrifices for sin, which are offered by the Law, 'thou hadst no pleasure'—no contentment, nor satisfaction; therefore you would have them no longer, says Christ to the Father; but 'a body thou hast prepared me. Then said he, Lo, I come to do thy will', by which will, viz. done and accomplished by him, we are sanctified (freed from sin and consecrated to the service of God), by the offering of the body of Jesus Christ once for all (cf. *Heb.* 10). Now, it's a great consolation to us: we are not to make a purchase by doing the will

of God; we are not to obey as though paying a price for our inheritance—that's done already. By faith we simply receive, and by obedience walk worthy of (or 'according to') the kingdom and glory to which we are called by our Lord Jesus Christ in the gospel.

2. Doing the will of God here, if you take it for works only, is not that by which we are justified, but rather that which justifies that we are justified; and by which our faith is made perfect—as the apostle says concerning Abraham (cf. *James* 2:22). It is not obedience which gives us our title to heaven, but rather it proves that we have a title given to us.

3. As to such things as we would do, but cannot, God will accept the will for the deed—provided we be as willing to do as to will the deed. Thus Abraham is said to have offered up his son because he was willing to

do it. And this is the consolation the apostle had, when to will was present with him, but he had no power to do—that with his mind he served the law or the will of God (cf. *Rom.* 7). The saints cannot do the things that they would because the flesh 'lusteth against the Spirit (*Gal.* 5:17). In such a case, Christ excuses his disciples with this, 'The spirit indeed (note that, 'spirit indeed') is willing, but the flesh is weak (*Matt.* 26:41). It is upon this account that Christ tells his Father that his disciples have kept his word, though they had failed very often, because their heart was in it (*John* 17:6).

4. By doing the will of God here is not to be understood such an exactness as will exclude any failings; that if a man should fall short in anything he will perish and be undone according to the law: 'cursed be he that confirmeth not all the words of this law to do them' (*Deut.* 27:26). Or, as

the apostle quotes it (*Gal.* 3:10), 'Cursed is every one that continueth not in all things which are written in the book of the law to do them.' We are free from this rigour and curse by Christ Jesus—he being made a curse for us (*Gal.* 3:13). But what is required of us is a continual care of doing, and making it our business to do, the will of God. As Christ says (*Matt.* 7:13), 'Enter in at the strait gate.' Yes, it is easily said 'enter in', but what is meant by this? Luke (as I said before) expounds it thus, 'Strive to enter in at the strait gate' so that striving is put for entering, because such shall enter.

The Apostle Peter with respect to this kingdom, expresses the duty as giving all diligence *(2 Pet.* 1:10-11):

> Wherefore the rather, brethren, give dili-
> gence to make your calling and election
> sure: for if ye do these things ye shall
> never fall: for so an entrance shall be

ministered to you abundantly, into the everlasting kingdom of our Lord and Saviour, Jesus Christ.

5. I add that God has promised his assistance to such ones so that though the work is too hard for us, yet through Christ strengthening us we may be able to do all these things. Therefore, when the apostle writes 'Work out your salvation with fear and trembling', he adds by way of encouragement: 'God worketh in you both to will and to do.' God will not be wanting to us, if we be not wanting to ourselves: God will bless the diligent hand. This will suffice for the doctrinal part.

The Application:

I come now to the Application and here there are three words or headings that I have to speak on. And, by the way, having spoken of three words let me address an unjust blame often laid on ministers for saying they have 'but a word or two more'. A 'word' in Scripture often means a heading or topic—The Ten Commandments are themselves called ten 'words:' 'God spoke these ten words, saying...' They are more than ten words and rather ten headings. Therefore let no one be foolish, laughing at the ministers who say, 'just a word more,' though they go on to speak longer!

These, then, are the three words or headings which I must address:

1. Information
2. Examination
3. Exhortation

1. Information:

i) The first is information of these truths and the first deduction or inference (call it what you wish) from the text is this: that very few will go to heaven. This very doctrine was preached by Christ upon this question. Some said to him, 'Are there few that be saved?' (*Luke* 13:23). He said in answer, 'Strive to enter, for many shall seek, and shall not be able;' and it is 'not every one that says to me "Lord, Lord" that shall enter heaven, but he that doth the will of my Father.' From this I infer—as Christ says—that there are but few, a very few, that will go to heaven. I beseech you, beloved, look about you and take it to heart. It is not such a common thing to be saved as the world thinks it is.

Read but a few scriptures and judge for yourself whether many or few will be saved—I mean in comparison to those who will be lost. In 1 Corinthians 6:9–10 Paul writes, 'Know ye not that the unrighteous shall not inherit the kingdom of God?' The 'unrighteous': that is a large word! Who are they? 'Be not deceived, neither fornicators (and are none of you such?), nor adulterers (and are none of you such?), nor the effeminate, nor abusers of themselves with mankind, nor thieves, nor the covetous (and are none of you such?), no, nor drunkards,' he writes (and are none of you such?). 'Be not deceived', none of these, no, not one of these living and dying thus, shall inherit the kingdom of God. Sad! Lord, what will become of this sinful world? If we should go throughout this City and separate the above named sinners, alas how few would remain to be saved!

Read also in Galatians 5:19 and following verses: 'Now the works of the flesh are manifest, which are adultery, fornication, uncleanness, lasciviousness, idolatry, witchcraft, hatred, variance,[12] emulations,[13] wrath, strife, seditions, heresies, envyings, murders,

---

[12] quarrelling
[13] jealousy

drunkenness, revellings and such like.' Does not the whole world almost lie in some or other of these? Is this not the fruit it brings forth? Well, what becomes of them? The apostle tells us in verse 21: 'Of the which I tell you before, as I have told you in time past: that they which do such things shall not,' no, 'they shall not, enter into the kingdom of God.'

Beloved, what do we think will become of us? Are these things just a tale that is told to us? How can we dare to say that we believe these scriptures and yet walk in these sins? If men believed that sin were a soul-damning thing, would they be so prodigal as to sin away their souls to hell? Do men love themselves no better than to damn themselves? Do not be deceived, the Scripture is true and will be found true in the day of judgement, and what will poor sinners do in that day?

See yet again in Ephesians: 'For this ye know that no whoremonger, nor unclean person, nor covetous man (what, take note I beg you, what bouts the Scripture has at the covetous man. He is always reckoned top among the worst of sinners) — such shall have no inheritance in the kingdom of Christ or of God. Let no man then deceive you with vain words, for because of these things cometh the wrath of God upon the children of disobedience' or unbelief (*Eph.* 5:5–6). Now, to leave the rabble and common sort of sinners in the world and look a little into the more refined sort of men, the professing world (how little is that!), and among professors. Let us separate those that have but a form of godliness and deny the power of it, holding the truth of God in unrighteousness; and those that in words confess him, and in works deny him. Separate the formalists and the hypocrites, and then judge if there be not few that shall be saved.

I think, beloved, it might make our hearts ache within us and it is strange that our countenances are not changed; that our faces do not become pale, that our thoughts are not troubled (like Belshazzar's) so that the 'joints of our loins' are 'loosed' and our knees knock one against the other (cf. *Dan.* 5:6), when we hear how few are like to go to heaven: none but they that do the will of God. And Lord, good Lord, how few are they? But:

ii) If it be so, then certainly it is men's greatest concern to do the will of God: to believe and live the gospel truths—unless they think it is an indifferent thing whether they go to heaven or hell; whether their souls be saved or damned. Let us 'up and be doing' lest we be undone. And if we have hitherto merely dallied with God and said,

'I'm going' but haven't gone, let us undo the evil we have done and do what it is we have neglected to do, by repenting. Indeed, we need such hindsight as repentance is who have brought ourselves so low by our past folly. He that repents that he has not done, is said to do his Father's will (cf. *Matt.* 21:31). That is, when the repentance is such as is not only for, but from dead works, and brings forth fruit i.e. amendment of life, serving God out of choice, and doing his will with pleasure. If God's will is not done, we shall be undone.

Christ tells us plainly, that unless our righteousness (our practical righteousness) exceeds the righteousness of the scribes and Pharisees, we shall not enter the kingdom of heaven (cf. *Matt.* 5:20). And yet, these men were beautiful externally, they outwardly appeared righteous; indeed, so righteous that it was an ordinary saying among the Jews that if only two men went to heaven, one would be a scribe and the other a Pharisee. Paul was a Pharisee and, concerning the law, blameless, yet he would not be found in that righteousness for all the world—it was but dung to him! His whole soul went after this: to be found in Christ Jesus and to have the righteousness which is through the faith of Christ, the righteousness which is of God by faith (cf. *Phil.* 3:9).

And take note of what influence this had upon his practice, such that he could propose it to all men as an example. For, he says, 'Our conversation is in heaven' (*Phil.* 3:20). He lived in this world as a man of another world and therefore, when he was ready to be offered, and the time of his departure was at hand, he could triumph in this: that he had fought a good fight, finished his course, kept the faith. And he says,

'there is laid up for me a crown of righteousness, which the Lord the righteous
judge, shall give me at that day.' Oh the joy
and peace and hope that comes from that!
How great a matter is it then for men's present and future happiness to do the will of
God!

iii) There is a third inference which
is this: that if it is so that they—and only
they—that do the will of God shall enter
the kingdom of heaven, then it is certainly
another matter to be a Christian than
men usually think. It is not he that talks
about God but he that walks with God
that is the Christian. Alas, my beloved,
it is an easy thing to take up a name and
make a profession; to be of this or that
opinion; to unite oneself to this, that
or the other way of worship and disci-
pline; to be of this or that denomination.
This is easy. But where is the Christian

all this time? Our blessed Saviour tells us plainly that it will cost a man something more than all this to be a Christian. It is not enough to say, 'Lord, Lord': the whole frame and constitution of a man must be altered. There is self to be denied; world to be crucified; flesh to be put to death; sin to be subdued; and the will of God to be obeyed. And is all this a small matter? Religion is no idle speculation, nor a mere profession, form of godliness, or a round of duties. Rather, the life of religion lies in living it: in bringing the whole man (inward and outward) to the obedience of God.

Godliness is God-likeness and certainly there cannot be a greater derogation to God and the gospel; nothing can more reflect upon God than for men to take his name in vain, as they do whenever they take his name into their mouth but do not depart from iniquity. The Christian is a new creature, putting off the old man, which is corrupted by deceitful desires, being renewed in the spirit of a man's mind, and putting on the new man, which is created according to God in righteousness and true holiness. External reformation, without internal renovation, will never partake of salvation.

Our need of Christ:

If this is so, what need do we have of Jesus Christ? Firstly, that we may do, and secondly after we have done, the will of God.

a) What need do we have of Jesus Christ that we may do the will of God? Because without him we can do nothing, as he himself tells us (cf. *John* 15:5). To be 'a sinner' and to be 'without strength' are phrases of one and the same significance as is shown by comparing Romans 5 verse 6 with verse 8. The same apostle who told us he could by Christ strengthening him do all things (cf. *Phil.* 4:13), tells us also in 2 Corinthians 3:5: 'Not that we are sufficient of ourselves (and he doubles it) as of ourselves to think (much less do) any thing, but our sufficiency is of God.' Oh what need there is then of Christ Jesus, to enlighten and enliven, to quicken and strengthen us, that we may be able to do his will!

When the apostle had prayed that they might walk worthy of God to all well-pleasing in Colossians 1:10, he prays in verse 11, in relation to this, that they might be strengthened with all might according to his glorious power. That is, that power by which he is able to subdue all things unto himself, and by which he raised Christ from the dead. As the prayer is in Hebrews 13:20-21: 'Now the God of peace, that brought again from the dead our Lord Jesus... make you perfect in every good work to do his will, working in you that which is well-pleasing in his sight.' It is a good rule, that of Luther's, that 'We must always observe God commanding us with an eye to Christ.'[14] Keep the commands or do my will in Christ, or by Christ, for without him we can do nothing.

b) We do not only need Christ that we may do, but we need Christ also when we *have done* the will of God. We have need not only of patience, but of Christ, that after we have done the will of God, we may inherit the promise. My beloved, we are but unprofitable servants when we have done our duty, because we have done only our duty. Alas how much more then are we unprofitable when we have not done our duty! And if we sin, what do you think? Do we not have need of an advocate with the Father and such a one as—indeed, the

---

[14] Venning paraphrases Martin Luther's *Five Disputations*, I.42

very—Jesus Christ the righteous, who is the propitiation for our sins? I think and am confident that (let men talk as much as they please) when the best in the world come to die, they will say with the great Cardinal, 'It's safer':[15] it is safer to ground our hopes upon what Christ has done and suffered than upon what we have done. For, alas, our all is too little, our best is too bad, our most perfect obedience is too imperfect to rely upon! Indeed, I will add that it is the will of God we should do so, as is evident from 1 John 2:1-2.

Pursuing godliness:

Yet I infer this also, without detracting from or contradicting what I have already said, that Christ's doing the will of God does

[15] Possibly Cardinal Nicholas de Cues (1401-64). Cf. *On Genesis*, X.4: 'It is therefore safer in such matters not to deal in human conjecture but to search out divine testimony.'

not exclude (or exempt us from) our doing the will of God. Though he has done the will of God, yet we also are to do the will of God—though not to the same ends. Far be it from me to undervalue what Christ has done and suffered! I live by it! Yet I say this: God forbid, far be it from us, let it not—it must not by any means—be that any of us should think that the obedience of Christ frees us from obedience. On the contrary, it strongly engages us to it. 'I come to do thy will,' he says, and by that will we are sanctified, which he speaks of in John 17:19: 'For their sakes I sanctify myself, that they also may be truly sanctified.' *Enaletheia* being understood similarly to *alethos*: sanctified 'in truth' or 'by the truth'.

Shall we then live in sin because Christ has died for sin? Because Christ has fulfilled the righteousness of the law and delivered us from it by putting an end to righteousness by the works of the law, shall we neglect to do righteous works? Did Christ do his Father's will so that we might do our own? That we might live as we like? God forbid! Do not be deceived: notwithstanding what Christ has done, we may go to hell if we be found workers of iniquity.

Are we not his workmanship, created (that is, new created) for good works? Is not he that is of God made righteousness, sanctification and redemption from all iniquity for us? Can we think that he will take our sins from us and not take us from our sins? Beloved, let me tell you, Christ died as much to sanctify as he did to save you. Indeed, to sanctify that he might save you. Christ does not only deliver his people from eternal condemnation, but he delivers them also from a sinful way of life and to this end, that he may deliver them from eternal condemnation. This is the blessing with which he is sent to bless you: to turn you away from your iniquity.

The same grace that has appeared bringing salvation also teaches us to deny ungodliness and worldly lusts, but to live in godliness, righteousness and soberness in this present world (cf. *Titus* 2:12). And where grace's teaching has not been learned, grace's salvation will not be bestowed. Why not? Because he gave himself for us, that he might redeem us from all iniquity and purify for himself a special people, zealous to do good works. The apostle charges me in the name of our Lord and Saviour—as I will give account at his appearing—to speak, exhort and rebuke with all authority. If anyone despises this message, it is at his own peril. He will one day find out that it did concern him.

Let me tell you again that he is become the author of eternal salvation to them—and only to them—that obey him (cf. *Heb.* 5:9). Though he is the Saviour of all, salvation is specifically to those who believe (cf. *1 Tim.* 4:10). 'And these things', he says, 'command and teach.' In a word: though Christ's satisfaction, not our sanctification, is the ground of our justification, yet wherever he is justification, he is sanctification also. Otherwise, there could be no salvation, for as I told you before, I tell you still: 'Without holiness no one shall see the Lord.' I beg you to consider it.

A further point is this (which I should have mentioned before): if God's will must, then our will must not be done—the doing of God's will implies the denying of our own. Christ came not to do his own will but his Father's, i.e. not only his own will. We must not do ours at all, but do all according to God's will. Man should not lean on his own understanding but in all his ways acknowledge God (cf. *Prov.* 3:5-6). In the things of this life, we should not conform to the will of flesh and blood—including our own—nor do anything because it is our will, but rather because it is the will of God. Whatever you do, the apostle says, from the highest duty of grace to the lowest of nature, whether you listen, pray, buy, sell, eat or drink, do all—not only one or two things, or one or two kinds of things but all—to the glory of God. That is, to please God which is when his will is done.

Look to it, then, you who say, 'Today or tomorrow we will go into such a city', when you should say, 'If the Lord wills' we will do this or that (cf. *James* 4:13, 15). Woe to those who say, 'With our tongue we will prevail, our lips are our own, who is lord over us?' (*Psa.* 12:4) Alas poor souls! You are not your own: your souls are not yours; your bodies are not yours. They are bought with a price and therefore it is not self-will but God's will that you and they are to obey (*1 Cor.* 6:19-20). Man must not make his own will but God's will his counsellor and his rule. Do nothing but by leave and approval. When therefore they stand in competition, we should tell temptations and corruption: 'It is God's will that I should not do my own will.' The great strife between God and man is about the will, and men are enemies to God because they cannot have their way. But alas! We see that if our will is done, God's will not be, and then woe to us because we 'reward evil to our own souls.'

If it is so that they—and none but they—who do the will of God shall inherit the kingdom of heaven, how sad then will it be with those who die in their sins; those who go out of the world having done nothing in it but working iniquity? Oh the tragic, dismal condition of sinners at the Last Day when they shall hear their doom, 'Depart from me, ye cursed, into everlasting fire, prepared for the devil and his angels'! (*Matt.* 25:41). Oh that the hearing of it now may prevent the hearing of it then! Will it not be sad to be turned into hell with loads of wrath and vengeance upon your backs? For what have you treasured up, you who work iniquity, but wrath for the day of wrath? You shall have your portion with hypocrites and be torn in pieces with no one to deliver you; have your dwelling with everlasting burning, where there will be nothing but weeping and wailing and gnashing of teeth. Consider this, you who work iniquity, and 'kiss the Son, lest he be angry' (*Psa.* 2:12) and you perish everlastingly.

Oh, that sinners would lend their ear and listen at the hole, at the mouth of the bottomless pit! They might hear sinners crying, like Cardinal Wolsey, 'Oh, if we had but taken as much care to please God as we did to please our own and other men's lusts, he would not have left us to this shame and endless misery!' There they might hear Dives crying out, 'I am tormented in this flame and have not so much as one little drop of water to cool my tongue' (cf. *Luke* 16:24). There they may hear poor, damned souls cursing themselves for their madness: that for the pleasures of sin (which are but for a moment), they should lose the pleasures of heaven and be under the torments of hell which are forever. Alas! It is not possible to express the unspeakable, the inconceivable miseries which the fearful and unbelieving—the workers of iniquity— will be in, when they shall be cast into and have their part in the lake which burns with fire and brimstone, where they shall be tormented day and night forever and ever. This is the second death (cf. *Rev.* 20:10; 21:8).

Oh that men would hear and fear, and no longer act so wickedly!

Lastly, if it be so, how happy shall they be who, when their Lord comes, shall be found doing the will of God! Well-doing will meet with a 'Well done, good and faithful servant: enter into the joy of your Lord!' Saints are called to God's kingdom and glory here, and called upon to walk 'worthy of', 'according to' or 'as befits' that kingdom, and when they have walked like this with God, they shall be called into the kingdom and glory. They shall hear the joyful sound saying, 'Come, you who are blessed by my Father: inherit the kingdom prepared for you.' They shall then sit down with Abraham, Isaac and Jacob at the wedding dinner, which is yet to be held in heaven, when all the saints gather together. Oh, what a glorious and blessed time that will be, when those who are now laughed at or scorned for being so religious, for doing the will of God, shall then be crowned with everlasting glory! Then you will see the distinction between the righteous and the wicked and between the one who serves God and the one who does not.

Now indeed, too many say in works and in their hearts, if not in words, 'It is pointless to serve God; what profit is there in keeping his commands? The proud are happy etc.' But the day is coming that will burn like an oven and all the proud and all that act wickedly will be like dry straw. But a book of remembrance is written before him of those who fear the Lord and think on his name, and for them shall the Sun of righteousness rise with healing in its wings (cf. *Mal.* 3:16; 4:2); and 'they shall be mine in that day, when I make up my jewels,' says the Lord (cf. *Mal.* 3:17). Yes, the Beloved of their souls and he who loves their souls will speak and say:

Rise up, my love, my fair one, and come away. For, lo, the winter is past, the rain is over and gone; the flowers appear on the earth, the time of the singing of birds is come, and the voice of the turtle [dove] is heard in our land; the fig tree putteth forth her green figs, and the vines with the tender grape give a good smell. Arise, my love, my fair one, and come away. Oh my dove, that art in the clefts of the rock, in the secret places of the stairs, let me see thy countenance, let me hear thy voice; for sweet is thy voice and thy countenance is comely! (*Song of Sol.* 2:10-14).

Though you have 'lain among the pots', you will be like the wings of a dove covered with silver, or her feathers covered with gold (cf. *Psa.* 68:13). Such, and much more than this, will be their glory. Indeed, eye has not seen nor ear heard, nor can it enter the heart of man to conceive the things which

God has prepared for those who love him
(cf. *1 Cor.* 2:9).

2. *Self-Examination:*

The second word, or heading, is for self-
examination and self-testing (and I wish
that such catechizing was more commonly
used). By this we may know whose we are
and what will become of us for eternity;
whose we are while we live, and whose we
shall be, and where we shall go when we die.
This, I think, should take up men's thoughts
and direct them day and night until they
were in some measure of assurance. And
oh, that men would often ask their souls
whose work, whose will they are doing. By
this they may conclude what their eternal
state will be.

Look, as men sow in the seed-time of
their lives, they shall reap in the harvest of
eternity. Can men expect to gather grapes

from thorns or figs from thistles? Oh no, 'Be not deceived,' mistake not yourselves. 'God is not mocked, for whatsoever a man soweth, that shall he also reap. For he that soweth to his flesh shall of the flesh reap corruption; but he that soweth to the Spirit shall of the Spirit reap life everlasting' (*Gal.* 6:7-8). And, says the apostle, 'Know assuredly that to whom ye yield yourselves as servants to obey, his servants ye are to whom ye obey, whether of sin unto death, or of obedience unto righteousness, that is, unto life' (cf. *Rom.* 6:16). He that is now your Lord and Master, he that is now your Sovereign and King, will then pay your wages.

It is a short question, 'Whose will are you doing?' If it is the will of men, you have your reward. If the will of sin, you shall have sin's wages, which is (you may hear it but how will you bear it?) eternal death. Surely, men that like sin's work will not like sin's wages. But if you do the will of God, your wages will be his gift: eternal life. Well then, for God's sake and that of your soul, test yourself that you may know whose you are and whose you shall be.

3. Exhortation:

The third word or heading is 'exhortation.' Let everyone that names and calls upon the name of the Lord, as he loves his own soul, leave iniquity behind. Alas if you do not depart from iniquity for God's sake, you must—there's no remedy—you must depart from God for iniquity's sake. Will sin be dearer to you than God and your own soul? 'Why do you call me Lord, Lord?' Let's either lay aside the name of the Lord or our iniquity. What are you doing, bold, impudent, daring sinner, taking God's name in your mouth but hating to be reformed? Do you think he will hold you guiltless if you take his name in vain? No, he will require his name and glory at your hands. Because God keeps quiet, do you think he gives you his consent? Do you think that he is like you? No, he will rebuke you and set your sins in order in front of you, and ask you how you dare say 'Lord, Lord' by way of profession, prayer and appeal and yet would not depart from iniquity. What will you answer when he rises up? You will stand speechless then, as one who is self-condemned.

Let me then beseech you to do the will of God. Do not be hearers of the word only, but doers also, so that you do not deceive yourselves (cf. *James* 1:22). What is it to make a good profession and not to make good the profession? What is it to be a Christian as far as—if no further than—a few good words will go? What is it to speak well of Christ, to say, 'Hail, Master' and kiss him, if you kick against him with your heel? Do not trust in lying words which cannot profit you. 'Will you steal, murder, commit adultery, swear falsely, burn incense to Baal and walk after other gods—your stomach and your covetousness—and then come and stand before me in this house and say "The temple of the LORD, the temple of the LORD, the Temple of the LORD is this?" Is this house which is called by my name, become a den of robbers in your eyes? Behold, says God, even I have seen it, and will require it' (cf. *Jer.* 7:9, 4, 10, 11). Good words will never engage God to be a patron to bad works.

Do you think you can lean upon the Lord and say, 'Is not the Lord among us?' Behold, you are called a 'Jew', and you depend upon the law, and make your boast of God and know his will. Behold, what will all this come to? If you, through breaking the law, dishonour God and cause his name to be blasphemed, what will you do in that day, when God shall judge you according to this gospel? (cf. *Rom.* 2:16–18, 23–4).

My beloved, let me beg you for your precious and immortal soul's sake, not to dally with God; not to trifle away these few moments of your life, upon which eternity depends. Be up and doing the will of God, that it may go well with you forever. It is said of some that they feared the Lord, but served their own gods (cf. *2 Kings* 17:33). But, the text says in verse 34, 'They feared not God, for they do not after the commandments which God commanded Jacob.' Alas my beloved, how often must I say it: it is not a form of godliness, it is not saying 'Lord, Lord', it is not quaint civility, nor baseless morality, much less painted hypocrisy that will bear you out. Opinions will not pass for true religion in the day of judgement.

No, do not think to make Christ a pack-horse: to lay your sins upon his shoulders, and in the meantime to keep them in your heart; to say he has done the will of God, and you don't care to do his will. Alas, the loss will be your own—God will lose nothing. Just as he that is wise is wise for himself, so he that sins wrongs his own soul. Be exhorted then, and accept this word of exhortation, which speaks thus: do the will of God, surrender, resign yourselves to him, if you expect to enter into the kingdom of heaven.

Why should we heed this exhortation?

There are two substantial arguments:

1. It is for no less than a kingdom—indeed, no less than the kingdom of heaven—and is that worth nothing? The gospel is called the gospel of the kingdom (cf. *Matt.* 4:23), and the word of the

kingdom (cf. *Matt.* 13:19), for by it we are called to his kingdom and glory. Will not a kingdom and, of all kingdoms, this kingdom be glorious in our eyes, which is the kingdom of glory? The devil offered Christ the kingdoms of this world and their glory as his greatest argument by which he hoped to prevail. But what is that to this? What is time to eternity? What is earth to heaven? What are visible things to invisible? What are the things of sense to things of faith? What is this glory to that which is to be revealed?

We all naturally love greatness and glory, and can there be any greater glory or more glorious greatness than this? To be kings to God here, kings with God hereafter and to reign with him more than a thousand years? You see what is done in the world (and I wish there were no evil done in the world) for crowns, sceptres, and kingdoms. Do not all the kingdoms of the earth suffer violence and do not the violent take them by force, and shall not the kingdom of God suffer violence seeing it suffers willingly? (cf. *Matt.* 11:12). Oh that the violent would take it by force! The nature of this kingdom is to keep you from evil; the kingdoms of the earth are not (I fear) had without much evil. Well, will you consider this to engage you to do the will of God? It is for a kingdom.

2. Consider this argument, also: if you neglect it today, it may be too late tomorrow. Now or never, now or never! For what is your life but as a vapour that passes away? Don't you die daily? Don't you know that this night you may sleep the sleep of death? And truly, my beloved, if you do not hear God in this, God will not hear you in that day of judgement. Many shall say in that day, 'Lord, Lord' but it will be too late. See

how Luke expands upon this: 'Strive'- do your utmost—'to enter in at the narrow gate, for many will (busily, with 'wouldings' and 'wishings') seek to enter, but will not be able to' (cf. *Luke* 13:24). He adds additional force by this argument. When the master of the house has risen up, and has shut the door, and you are standing outside and begin to knock, saying, 'Lord, Lord, open to us,' he shall answer and say to you, 'I don't know you or where you are from' (cf. *Luke* 13:25). 'It is too late,' he will say: 'There was a door of hope open, but now it is shut.' Then you would not, now you will not enter. Though you cry and shout, he will shut out your cries. Indeed, though you cry, 'Lord, Lord,' his answer will be, 'I don't know you.'

And if you begin to plead and say, 'How, Lord, not know us? That's strange! Not know us!' 'Why, who are you that I should know you?' As he says in Matthew, 'I never knew you.' 'No, Lord? We have eaten and drunk in your presence. We have heard you preach in our streets. We were the greatest attendees of sermons in the whole town or county. And you don't know us?' 'No' Christ will say, 'I don't know you.' Well, in Matthew they have something more to say for themselves. 'We have prophesied in your name. Indeed, we have fought your battles and cast out devils, and in your name have done many wonderful works. Is not this enough to be known by? Surely you can't but have taken notice how forward we were in and for your cause!' But, alas, the answer is 'I never knew you, depart; depart, I don't know you.'

Oh, beloved, it may be we think that we are known now, well known, but if we are found to be workers of iniquity, it will be in vain to say—when we knock and God says, 'Who is there?'—here are those who sat in the upper end of the world. Here are famous citizens, council men, even alder- men of the City of London.[16] Alas, we shall never be known under these labels, upon such terms. It is not riches, nor titles of honour by which men are known in this world, that will make a man known of God when he comes to stand before the bar of his tribunal.

God will invalidate all the pleas that can be made. If you say, 'When did we see him hungry or thirsty, a stranger, naked, or in prison, or sick and did not minis- ter to him?' He will answer, 'Depart, you who are cursed, for in as much as you did not do it for one of the least of these, you did not do it for me' (cf. *Matt.* 25:44-5). If you say, 'Open to us, for we are virgins, we took our lamps and went out to meet the

---

[16] Many of those listening to the sermon would have fallen into these categories. One can imagine the impact.

bridegroom, the rest slept as much as we did; we trimmed our lamps and because we could not borrow, we went to buy. Lord, Lord, open to us!' 'No, truly,' he will say, 'I don't know you' (cf. *Matt.* 25:11-12).

The day of judgement will be a dreadful day upon this account—that it will be a day of deceit. Not that it will deceive anyone, but many will find that they themselves have been deceived. Oh, how many will be frustrated in their expectations! It will be for them as it was for Esau on the day when Jacob was blessed. He came in happy from his hunting and said (without doubting he would be successful), 'Bless me, my father.' But it was too late. He sought it, yes, desperately sought it with tears, but found no place for repentance. His father would not recall the blessing.

If men will not hear when God calls, there is a time coming when men shall call and God will not hear. How greatly does Christ mourn over Jerusalem, who so long neglected her own peace that at last it was hidden from her? 'It's too late, it's too late, Jerusalem!' Oh therefore in this day, in this your day, in this the day of your own visitation by God; today, while it is called today, before the night of death comes—and that may be this night, even—I say to you in this day: hear his voice or else in that day he will not hear your voice, though you cry out, 'Lord, Lord, open to us!'

Concluding exhortations:

In conclusion, there are three things which I would commend to you briefly in relation to this great matter. If they—and none but they—shall enter into heaven but those who do the will of God on earth, let me entreat you to take note of:

1. The *what* of God's will

2. The *how* of God's will

3. The *why* of God's will

1. Study what the will of God *is*, that is, the things to be believed and done. Do not rest content with a general notion, but study from the Scriptures what the will of God is in particular. Noteworthy advice is given—and a noteworthy promise made—in Proverbs 2:1-5:

> My son, if thou wilt receive my words, and hide my commandments with thee; so that thou incline thine ear unto wisdom, and apply thine heart to understanding; yea, if thou criest after knowledge, and liftest up thy voice for understanding; if thou seekest her as silver, and searchest for her as for hid treasures (what then?), then shalt thou understand the fear of the LORD and find the knowledge of God.

And that not only in general but, as in verse 9: 'then shalt thou understand righteousness, and judgement, and equity,' indeed, 'every good path.'

Can there be a matter of greater concern to us than the saving of our souls? Can we take too much care to that end? Is it not a shame that men should be more industrious in seeking to be wise for this world, than to be wise for heaven? Surely God requires us to be diligent and also to delight in this endeavour.

Every verse above has a double charge: verse 1, 'receive' and 'hide'; verse 2, 'incline thy ear' and 'apply thine heart'; verse 3, 'cry' and 'lift up the voice'; verse 4, 'seek her' and 'search for her as for silver and gold.' Ah, how much do we seek after silver and gold! Certainly if we looked after the will of God, as we do after silver and gold, how rich would we be in knowledge! What treasures of wisdom would our souls possess! We need not doubt it, for our Saviour has said it: 'if any man will do his will, he shall know of the doctrine, whether it be of God' (*John* 7:17). Therefore, do not be unwise but understand what the Lord's will is (cf. *Eph.* 5:17).

2. Study the *how* of the will of God—not only what is to be done but how it is to be done. It is not enough that we do what is good, but the good we do must be done well: his will being done according to his will. The apostle prays, in relation to walking worthy of God to all well-pleasing, that they might be filled with the knowledge of his will—and that in all wisdom and spiritual understanding; that they might know not only what to do, but how and when to do it (cf. *Col.* 1:9-10). The Hebrews have a saying that, 'God is more delighted in adverbs than in nouns.' It is not so much the thing done, as the manner of doing it—its various requisite qualities—with which God is concerned: not how much but how

well. It is not merely a good act that God requires of us, but that this act be done well, that our good deed may not be turned into evil and our holy things into sin.

3. Thirdly—and lastly—let me beseech you to study the *why* of the will of God. What is the end of all our actions? Why should we do the will of God? To please him: not merely to please ourselves but to please him. We should not seek our own good and salvation, as though to serve God only that we might serve ourselves by him. The great thing before our eyes should be that which was before Christ's: not only to do the things that please him, or only to do them so that they may be pleasing, but to do them in order to please him. 'This,' Paul says in 2 Corinthians 5:9, 'is our ambition'—so we may read it—'that we may be (we read it 'accepted by him' but I would rather read it in the active voice) acceptable

to him,' which is the way Paul expresses it in Romans 14:8. Whether we live we live to him, or whether we die we die to him. Whether it be life or death, all I aim at is that he may be magnified or glorified.

I shall conclude all that I have written as Christ concludes this very discourse: 'Therefore, whosoever heareth these sayings of mine and doth them, I will liken him to a wise man, who built his house upon a rock. The rain descended, the floods came, the winds blew, and they (they all) beat upon that house.' They fell upon it with all their force and violence, but it did not fall for it was founded upon a rock: even that against which the gates of hell shall not prevail. 'But every one that heareth these sayings of mine and doth them not, shall be likened unto a foolish man, who built his house upon the sand. The rain descended, the floods came, the winds blew, and (as before) beat upon that house.' However the word is not the same, nor does it signify the same force as previously. Rather, they 'stumbled' on that house, or only 'kicked at' that house, but down it fell without further ado, and great was its fall (*Matt.* 7:27). I wish better for you. That is, that now you have heard, you may do the word and will of God, which you may do and be blessed.

The God of peace that brought again from the dead our Lord Jesus Christ, the great shepherd of the sheep, through the blood of the everlasting covenant, make you perfect in every good work to do his will, working in you that which is well-pleasing in his sight, through Jesus Christ, to whom be glory forever and ever, Amen (cf. *Heb.* 13:20-21).

OTHER
POCKET PURITANS

Also by Ralph Venning…

The Sinfulness of Sin
Puritan Paperback

Here is a crystal-clear explanation of what sin is, why it is so serious and what we need to do about it.

ISBN: 978 0 85151 647 9

paperback | 284 pp.

Learning in Christ's School
Puritan Paperback

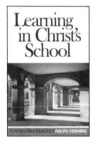

In this unique account of growth in grace, 'babes', 'little children', 'young men' and 'fathers' are the four stages through which the learners in Christ's school pass before they enter the 'academy of heaven'.

ISBN: 978 0 85151 764 3

paperback | 304 pp.

Available from your local Christian bookshop, or from

www.banneroftruth.org